BAHAMIAN LOYALISTS
AND THEIR SLAVES

GAIL SAUNDERS

CARIBBEAN

First published 1983
Reprinted 1984, 1987

Published by *Macmillan Publishers Ltd*
London and Basingstoke
Associated companies and representatives in Accra,
Auckland, Delhi, Dublin, Gaborone, Hamburg, Harare,
Hong Kong, Kuala Lumpur, Lagos, Manzini, Melbourne,
Mexico City, Nairobi, New York, Singapore, Tokyo

ISBN 0 333 35831 7

Printed in Hong Kong

To Winston

Contents

Foreword

It is most appropriate that a book about the Loyalists and their slaves should be written. Both the Loyalists and their slaves have had a profound impact on the social, economic and political life of The Bahamas.

Mrs Gail Saunders has shown a keen interest in Bahamian history for many years. She heads the Government's Department of Archives; she is an active member of The Bahamas Historical Society; and she is the Society's First Vice-President and editor of its annual Journal. She has lectured at home and abroad on Bahamian history researched from the records.

Mrs Saunders' work is a brief but valuable contribution to Bahamian history of the period in question. As accurately as she can, she has documented the role played by the Loyalists and their slaves in the development of our country. I should like to congratulate her and wish her every success in her venture.

Rt Hon. Sir Lynden O. Pindling
Prime Minister

Acknowledgements

Any book owes its production to many people. I am most indebted to Miss Patrice Williams for checking for historical accuracy, David Wood for the reproduction of most of the photographs and Mrs Bernice Kelly and Mrs Alexis Pearce for their invaluable assistance. Thanks is also due to Mr Tex Turnquest for drawing the maps, to Mr Alton Lowe for his general assistance with the manuscript and photographs and to Mr Winston Saunders for reading and commenting on the manuscript. A special thanks is owed to the Rt Honourable Prime Minister for agreeing to write the Foreword.

I should like also to thank the staff of the Department of Archives for supplying materials and for their moral support. I owe gratitude to my family especially my parents, Mr and Mrs E. Basil North and my parents-in-law, Mr and Mrs Harcourt Saunders for their continued help and encouragement.

My deepest thanks is owed to my husband Winston Saunders for his patience, support and sound advice.

Photograph acknowledgements
The author and publishers wish to acknowledge, with thanks, the following photographic sources:
Courtesy of Steven Brennen, Learning Resources Unit, Ministry of Education and the Department of Archives, Nassau p 62
Courtesy of Donald Cartwright p 53(bottom)

Preface

This small book was written as a part of the effort to commemorate the two hundredth anniversary of the coming of the Loyalists and their slaves to the Bahamas between 1783 and 1800. I should like to pay a special tribute to Thomas Wardle IV who along with Alton Lowe gave me the idea. It was Thomas Wardle's persistence that I speak to the Monarchist League of Canada and the Governor Simcoe Branch of the United Empire Loyalists' Association of Canada on the subject of Bahamian Loyalists that forced me to review some of my writing on the subject. Alton Lowe further encouraged me especially in his dedicated effort to make the Memorial Sculpture Garden, which is due to be opened in the Autumn of 1983, a reality. I should also like to commend James Mastin and Sandra Riley for their help in the project.

Bahamian Loyalists and their Slaves is based mainly on research I completed in the late 1970s for my M.Phil. Thesis on 'The Slave Population in the Bahamas 1783-1834'. Although this is only a brief excerpt with many amendments, I feel that it would be remiss of me not to mention my Master's Supervisor, Dr Barry Higman who gave me such careful guidance, and Professor Michael Craton, under whom I am now working as a doctoral candidate.

I have tried in a short space to trace the Loyalist settlements and the influence that they had on the Bahamas' development. Although much more research is needed, I have attempted to give insight into a neglected but important subject — The Slaves of the Loyalists. The Slaves, who were in the majority, had a profound impact on Bahamian history. However, in a book such as this one, I have merely scraped the surface.

Gail Saunders
August, 1982
NASSAU

[1]

Loyalist Population & Settlement in the Bahamas

UST AS THE CAUSES OF THE AMERICAN Revolution were complex, so were the contesting groups involved. The conflict was not a straight battle between Americans and the British. The colonists themselves were divided.[1] In fact Dr Wallace Brown went as far as to call it more of a civil war than the 1861-1865 hostilities.[2]

The origins of the division which produced Loyalism in the American society of the period is difficult to pin-point but the Stamp Act Crisis of 1765 probably saw a beginning. It was the Declaration of Independence in July 1776 however, which demarcated the Whigs from the Tories or Loyalists. The former were for the establishment of an independent Republic, the latter opposed independence and favoured reconciliation with Great Britain.

Why people chose to remain Loyalists is difficult to explain. Wallace Brown contends that most Loyalists thought that the break with Britain would lose them something material or spiritual.[3] Some feared the loss of their jobs, trade, prestige, and the Anglophiles, the Empire. Many were alienated from Whiggish circles; some thought the British were invincible; many opposed independence but some simply followed their leaders.[4]

The persecution of the Tories which began in earnest after 1774 was terrible. Each State passed legislation requiring inhabitants to take oaths to the new United States or be deemed

1

traitors. Some Loyalists had their property confiscated; others were socially ostracised and their businesses boycotted. All types of atrocities in the name of patriotism were inflicted against the Loyalists, the most infamous and common being that of tarring and feathering.

Loyalists were fined, pressured socially, mobbed and deprived of earning a living and some were banished. Others left voluntarily, initially finding sanctuary within the British lines, especially in East Florida. Formerly a Spanish Colony, East Florida was ceded to Britain after the Seven Years' War and was favoured by the Southern Loyalists, especially those from Georgia and the Carolinas. Later they left the country altogether.

Estimates calculate that between 80,000 and 100,000 Loyalists fled from the United States.[5] Some went to the West Indies, including Jamaica, Dominica and the Bahamas. A few went to Great Britain while the majority settled in Canada, especially in the Maritime Provinces, Ontario, and Quebec.

THE BAHAMAS BEFORE THE LOYALISTS

Before the coming of the Loyalists and their slaves the Bahamas were sparsely populated. According to contemporary accounts, the islands were thinly settled, the whole population amounting to between 4,000 and 5,000 people, a great proportion being free.[6] Except for New Providence, Eleuthera and Harbour Island, most Bahamian islands were as yet unsettled. If they were they had small populations. The inhabitants were very poor and owned little property, usually comprising a few small vessels and a few slaves. There was no plantation system as such.

Principally occupied in a sea-faring life of fishing, wrecking, turtling, the early inhabitants also engaged in woodcutting, mainly dye-woods and other varieties such as madeira and box-wood.

There was no staple crop and very little agriculture. The only produce was a little fruit with some easily-grown products such as guinea corn, peas, beans, potatoes, yams, plantains and bananas. The inhabitants took to rambling when the plantation soil failed. Schoepf, a German traveller described the older inhabitants of Nassau as amiable, courteous, hospitable and liking to drink and dance the time away.[7]

2

No sheep or cattle were raised and the diet comprised mainly fish, probably conch, turtle, iguanas and the above mentioned vegetables and fruit.[8] According to William Wylly, a Loyalist who became Attorney General of the islands, the total exports (which included wrecked goods, and probably salt and dye-woods) to Great Britain in 1773/1774 amounted to £5,216. 8. 10 and the imports to £3,581. 0. 0.[9] No account was kept of imports or exports to and from other countries.

Salt was raked and gathered by the settlers prior to the coming of the Loyalists, but was mainly for local consumption. In the late eighteenth and early nineteenth centuries, the main salt-producing islands were Turks Island, Exuma and Ragged Island.[10] Indeed, even before the American Revolutionary War and the coming of the Loyalists, salt was raked at Turks Island by the few resident inhabitants (Wylly estimated that there were eighteen white heads of families and forty slaves) and by visiting Bermudians who came to the island in the early part of the year to rake salt. Other islands of the British Caribbean such as Anguilla also supplied the Thirteen Colonies on the mainland with salt before 1776.

Nassau, the chief town located on the strategically-placed New Providence island, was a shabby little port overgrown with shrubs and trees. It comprised one narrow unpaved street, mostly wooden buildings and a few unimpressive public buildings. Schoepf described the now famous Bay Street, then the only tolerably regular street, as a narrow and shore-winding one which was lined with houses and shops on one side and an open harbour on the other. Vendue House, one of the public buildings where everything was sold, including slaves, was single-storied and arcaded and located at the bottom of George Street. Included among the other public buildings was a church (on the site of the present-day Christ Church Cathedral), a jail (on the eastern corner of what is now Market Street and Bay Street), and an assembly house. As yet the modern Government House on Mount Fitzwilliam did not exist.

Most houses and buildings in Nassau were of wood. According to Schoepf, chimneys were unknown and cooking was usually performed in a detached kitchen or shed. Glass windows existed, but were rare. Usually, solid window shutters were utilised in houses which had their own gardens.

3

Table to show the state of the population, agriculture etc. of the Bahama Islands in June, 1788

Principal islands on which there are settlements	White Male Heads of Families	Planters Possessing Ten or More Slaves	Merchants	Numbers of Slaves	Acres of Cultivated Land	Of the 3 Learned Professions	Further Remarks
New Inhabitants							
New Providence	165	27	26	1,264	3,060	16	
Exuma	26	19	–	679	2,591	–	
Long Island	29	19	–	476	2,380	–	
Cat Island	28	16	–	442	1,747	–	
Abaco	49	10	–	198	1,837	–	(Planters moving off)
Andros Island	22	7	–	132	813	–	Newly settled
Crooked Island	5	4	–	357	–	–	Ditto
Caicos	6	5	–	214	460	–	
Eleuthera, Harbour Island & Turks Island	–	–	–	–	–	–	
TOTAL NEW	330	107	26	3,762	12,888	16	

Old Inhabitants						
New Providence	131	3	1,024	255	1	
Exuma	11	–	75	354	–	
Long Island	42	12	306	1,530	–	Also 21 families of colour
Cat Island	12	–	16	250	–	
Abaco	–	–	–	–	–	
Andros Island	4	3	56	290	–	
Crooked Island	–	–	–	–	–	
Caicos	1	–	5	30	–	
Turks Island	18	–	40	–	–	
Harbour Island	94	–	142	–	–	
Eleuthera	119	–	310	725	–	The 310 slaves are mostly free people of colour
TOTAL OLD	430	3	1,974	3,434	1	
Majority of New Planters, etc.	0	13	1,790	9,454	15	
Majority of Old	100	–	–	–	–	
GENERAL TOTAL, both of Old & New	760	29	5,696	16,322	17	

Source: Wylly, W., *A Short Account of the Bahama Islands* (adapted) (London 1789) p.7

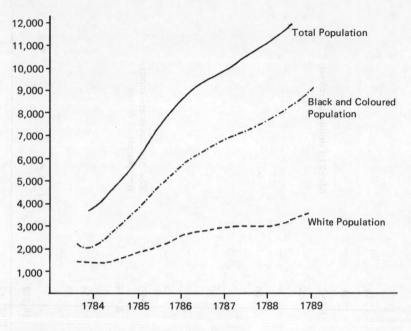

Estimate of population 1784–1789

Saunders. *The Slave Population of the Bahamas 1783–1834*. M.Phil. Thesis, University of the West Indies

LOYALIST SETTLEMENT

Colonel Andrew Deveaux Lieutenant-Colonel of the South Carolina Militia and then exiled in Florida, one of the last strongholds of Britain in the United States, received word that the Bahamas were suffering from being under the domination of Spanish rule. He determined to end this and took the Bahamas by force from the Spanish in February 1783.

Little did he and the other Loyalists who accompanied him, including volunteers both whites and slaves from Eleuthera and Harbour Island, know that the Treaty of Versailles on 10 February 1783 had ceded the Bahamas back to Britain and, alarmingly, East and West Florida to Spain. The East and West Floridian Loyalists therefore, desiring at all times to be under Britain, began their migration to the Bahamas, the West Indies (especially Jamaica) and Canada.

Not many Loyalists wished to come to the Bahamas at first, as

6

Colonel Andrew Deveaux

there was little information about conditions there. What they found out was not very promising. A report by Lewis Johnson and Lieutenant Wilson of the Engineers, who completed an extensive tour of the Bahama Islands, was not very favourable. Wilson described the soil as rocky but blamed the indolence of the inhabitants for the poor state of cultivation. He seem convinced however that the different types of Bahamian soils would grow cotton, vegetables and all kinds of guinea corn.[11]

Perhaps it was the arrival of some government transports and victuallers at St Augustine, East Florida in September 1783 and the prospects of favourable offers of grants of land to those who wished to settle in the Bahamas, rather than the report that gave impetus to the movement of Loyalists from East Florida to the Bahamas. It would once more uproot those Loyalists who had fled to Florida after the evacuation of Savannah and Charleston in July and December respectively in 1782 and of New York in 1783.

It is believed that most of the Loyalists arrived in the Bahamas

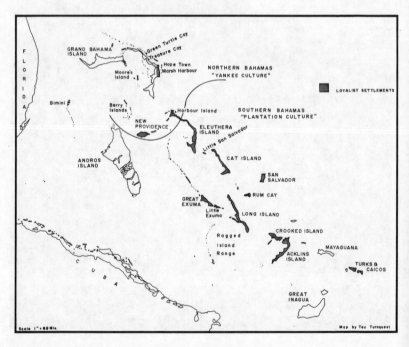

The Bahamas, showing Loyalist settlements between 1783 and 1788

between 1783 and 1785. They settled in most of the Bahamian Islands including New Providence, Abaco, Eleuthera, Exuma, Cat Island, Long Island, Crooked Island, Acklins, Watlings Island (now San Salvador), Turks and Caicos (which were then in the Bahamas). Wylly estimated that in 1788 the white inhabitants numbered 3,100, the slaves 5,696 and the people of colour 500, giving a total of 9,296. This did not include some others who were scattered on the smaller cays, probably about 350 people of colour, either free or pretending to be so. Some were runaways from the American States. With regard to the population, the Loyalists revolutionised the Bahamas.

According to Governor John Maxwell, who was under some pressure from some of the Loyalists, there were two classes of Loyalists — the farmers who settled on the Out Islands with large families and ten, twenty, or a hundred slaves, and the second group who were officers, merchants and professionals, many of whom wished to return to America when conditions settled down. The Governor praised the former group, but stated that nothing could satisfy the second group, his main critics, who found fault with the way he conducted business in general. He complained of their demanding behaviour and saw them as a threat.[12] The latter group settled mainly in New Providence and the Northern Bahamas. It is difficult to discern from the records exactly when and where all the Loyalists' Settlements took place. Perhaps the first were at Abaco and Cat Island.

One of the first references to a Loyalist settlement was in March 1784 when the Governor of the Bahamas, John Maxwell, wrote to the Secretary of State for the Colonies, Lord Sydney:

'A number of refugees from New York and St Augustine have repaired to several of the principal islands in this Government, where they have settled themselves; and one of them namely, Abaco, they have laid out a town, which they called Carleton.'[13]

Carleton, named after Sir Guy Carleton, British military commander of North America, stationed in New York, was located at the present-day Treasure Cay.[14] Other Loyalists settled around the same time at Marsh Harbour and Maxwell Town both in Abaco. Many of the blacks who arrived in Abaco at this time were in fact free. Those who settled at Marsh Harbour and the former Maxwell Town had quarrelled with their fellow-settlers at Carleton.

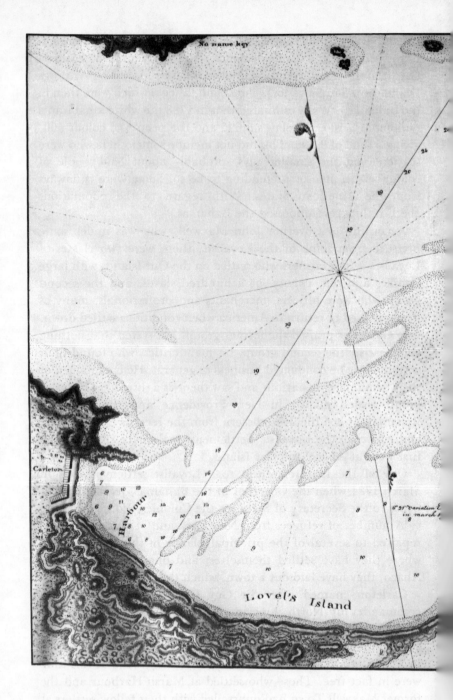

Early map showing the settlement of Carleton, Abaco

10 feet   7 fathoms

30

W H A L E K E Y.

INS. GENERAL OF FORTIFICATIONS

PLAN
of the Settlement and
Harbour
at
Carleton
On the Island of
ABACO
Surveyd By John Watson
Acting Engineer

Published August 11th 1784 by Wm ....

11

There were other small settlements established on the Abaco mainland and at Cat Island, and over the next two years an estimated 5,000 to 7,000 Loyalists and their slaves, encouraged by grants of land, migrated from Georgia and the Carolinas to the Bahamas. However, others stayed and were joined by migrants from Harbour Island, forming new towns, especially on the outer Cays exposed to the ocean and resources of the sea. Carleton and Maxwell Town disappeared. New Plymouth or Green Turtle Cay with its emphasis on fishing, wrecking and whaling, was soon the most important town in Northern Abaco. Today it is a picturesque village reminiscent of a New England port. Hope Town, further south, was founded by Wyannie Malone, a widow, with her four children who intermarried with Conchs. Hope Town had developed into a large and important settlement by the 1880s. Both New Plymouth and Hope Town boast private museums; the Albert Lowe Museum founded by Alton Lowe in Green Turtle Cay, and the Wyannie Malone Museum spearheaded by descendants of its founder including the late Byrle Patterson and her sisters, Shirley Higgs and Joan Albury.

Dr Thelma Peters demonstrated that there was a tinge of Yankeeism among those who settled in Abaco especially, and in the northern Bahamas in general, for example, North Eleuthera, Harbour Island and Spanish Wells.[15] Peters maintains that people who live in Abaco still possess the resourcefulness and independence often associated with Yankee Sailors. It is true that Abaconians still obtain their livelihood mainly from the sea. In fact a significant proportion of slaves in 1834 were listed in the Registers of the Return of Slaves as mariners. They fished and engaged in wrecking and trade with America.

Dr Peters also showed that the geography of the Bahamas was significant to the actual distribution of the Loyalists. The northern islands of Abaco, New Providence and North Eleuthera are more temperate and experience relatively cold winter spells while the southern islands are more tropical. She maintained that Abaco and the northern part of Eleuthera 'developed a cultural pattern quite alien to the so-called plantation islands to the South'.[16] In Abaco, she argued, the Loyalists either adjusted to a Bahamian way of life, enduring the hardships and learning the way of the sea, or they left the Bahamas. They also inter-married with the Conchs, in contrast to the majority of the Loyalists on

Modern day Green Turtle Cay

New Providence and the southern islands.

Among the Loyalists who settled and remained in the northern islands was the Curry family. Joseph Curry's five sons, Joseph, John, Richard, Benjamin and William, moved to the Bahamas from South Carolina after the Revolutionary war and inter-married with the Conchs. It is said that all the Currys in the Bahamas today can trace their ancestry to these brothers.

Those Loyalists who went south and south-east, settled islands which for the most part had few, if any, inhabitants. Such islands included Crooked, Acklins and Long Cay, Cat Island (which in 1783 and for most of the nineteenth century was referred to as San Salvador), Watlings, Rum Cay and the Exumas. The Loyalists, using slave labour and a staple crop pattern which they had known in Georgia and South Carolina, established cotton plantations.

Denys Rolle of East Florida was one of the principal settlers on Exuma, Charles Farquharson and Burton Williams were among those on San Salvador and William Moss, an owner of many slaves, settled on Crooked Island and Acklins. He owned several plantations including Prospect Hill Estate and the True Blue Estates on Crooked Island. True Blue has survived as a settlement on that island to this day. Duncan and Archibald Taylor settled at Ragged Island and the capital of the island is named after one of the brothers. Among those Loyalists who settled on Cat Island were Joseph and Oswell Eve, the former the inventor of a wind-turned cotton gin. However, most of the settlers had little aptitude and training for agriculture using the rocky and thin soil of the Bahama Islands.

New Providence in the strict sense was not a plantation island. Many of the Loyalists who settled there were business men, professionals and government officials. Quite a number of the plantation Loyalists who owned estates on the Out Islands bought business and residential properties in Nassau.

Dr Peters theorised that New Providence developed into a 'kind of physical and psychological bridge between the Yankee culture to the north and the plantation economy culture to the south'. It also served as the battlefield between the two groups.[17] A large proportion of southern planters lived in Nassau for at least a part of the year while their plantations were run by overseers. Among the eighty Loyalists described by Lydia Parrish in her unpublished manuscript, three were medical doctors, one a surgeon, one a cabinet maker, two ships' captains, one a mariner and one a school teacher — the latter doubling up as an auctioneer.

Prominent among the New Providence Loyalists were Adam Chrystie, Secretary of the Bahamas and a member of the Council; Stephen Delancey, Chief Justice (after whom Delancey Town is named); and William Wylly, a former captain in the Carolina Rangers. Wylly, who owned three plantations on New Providence including one at Clifton, quickly rose to the position of Attorney General and was perhaps the most controversial figure in Bahamian politics for a quarter of a century. John Wells, the first newspaper publisher in the Bahamas, also settled in Nassau and helped the Loyalists in their fight to gain political power.

Feuds developed not only between the Loyalists and the old inhabitants or Conchs (whom they considered inferior) together with the local colonial government headed by the Governor, but friction also raged between refugees from West Florida and the merchant-planters from East Florida. Most of the latter had close ties either of blood or friendship and were clannish. Some families, sought plantations in the same islands, for example, the Bellinger and Kelsall families who settled at Little Exuma.

In fact, those Loyalists from East Florida formed themselves into a Board of American Loyalists in 1784 to preserve their traditional liberties. Headed by James Hepburn and allied to the

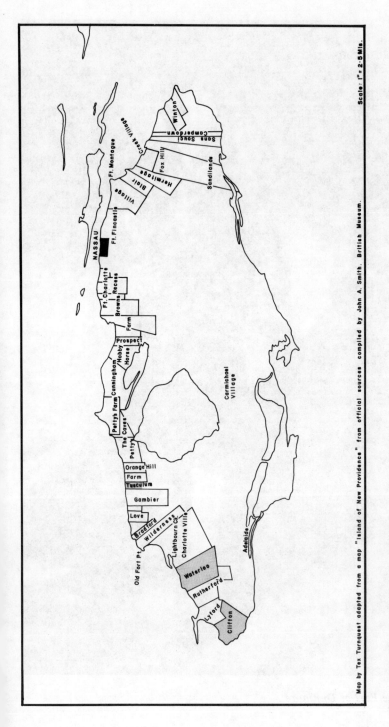

Map by Tex Turnquest adapted from a map "Island of New Providence" from official sources compiled by John A. Smith. British Museum.

Scale: 1" = 2.5 Mis.

New Providence, showing main estates in 1858

The Earl of Dunmore

trading company of Panton, Leslie and Company, the East Floridians opposed the existing government of the islands and gradually gained prominent government and political positions, causing much anguish to Colonial governors John Maxwell and the Earl of Dunmore.

The Loyalists and their slaves at least doubled the population of the Bahama Islands. In the economic sphere they attempted to introduce new crops, especially the growing of cotton. They brought development, even if on a modest scale, to many hitherto uninhabited or scarcely inhabited islands. Introducing a plantation economy in the south, they infused new life into the commercial activity of the islands.

Socially they introduced the concept of plantation life and a different kind of relationship between master and slave. By bringing so many slaves to the Bahamas, the Loyalists changed the social structure of the society and set down racial lines to be followed for centuries to come. They also influenced religious life and in fact influenced the whole tone of Bahamian life. Their contribution ranged from the introduction of innovative architecture to a lending library and the first newspaper. In the political area the Loyalists created factional feeling and challenged the older ruling Bahamian party.

[2]

The Slaves
of the Loyalists

HE SLAVE POPULATION BROUGHT BY the Loyalists was very important socially and economically to the Bahamas' growth. Numerically it increased the black population and put it in the majority. Slaves were used to build the plantation system, and when it failed, they were worked as field labourers on farms and were utilised as salt-rakers, seamen, domestics and artisans. Slaves were the necessary ingredient to the system that the Loyalists tried to construct, and their impact has been profound.

Research has shown that West Indian slaves had a life of their own, out of the jurisdiction of their masters. In fact they were one of the significant components in the creation of the creole society for which Edward Brathwaite argued.[18] His theory of slave society as distinctive; neither European nor African, but creole, a combination of two great traditions under the Jamaican environment, can be applied to the other British West Indies including the Bahamas. Indeed as historians such as Higman and Craton[19] have shown, slaves were still influenced by Africa but also shaped by the creole environment. Developing a unique set of values, British West Indian slaves possessed their own family patterns, modes of agriculture and had their own customs. Descendants of these slaves, who chiefly remained in the islands, eventually became the dominating force in West Indian life. The Bahamian descendants of the Loyalists' slaves were no exception.

Because of the scarcity of records very little is known about the identity or origin of the slaves who accompanied the Loyalists to the Bahamas. However, the Loyalists considered their slaves the most valuable property that they brought to the Bahamas.[20] From all accounts it seems that most of the slaves brought in by the Loyalists were creoles. Native-born blacks made up the majority of the slave population in the North American colonies as early as the late seventeenth century.[21] By the end of the American Revolutionary war, the African component of the black population had shrunk to twenty per cent. It is clear that the percentage of Africans in America was much less than in the British West Indies. Thirty-eight years after the advent of the Loyalists, the Returns of Registration of Slaves for the Bahamas gave listing of:

AFRICAN		CREOLE		TOTAL
Male	*Female*	*Male*	*Female*	
1,397	888	4,132	4,391	10,808

It seems that in 1822 with over four times as many Creoles as Africans, and a relatively high birth-rate of 18.40 per thousand and a relatively low death rate of 7.84, it was almost certain that more creole slaves had been brought in by the Loyalists than Africans. Generally over the Registration period from 1822 to 1834, the Bahamian slave population experienced a high rate of natural increase. This was due mainly to a creole slave population which was generally more fertile and less subject to mortality than the displaced Africans. The equalisation of sex-ratio and the large proportion of potential mothers in the slave population by 1822 also contributed towards the high birth rates.

Very few Africans were imported after 1790 and the ending of the slave trade in 1807 also had an important effect on the Bahamian slave population. Because of the decayed plantation system and the lack of the need to import further slaves, the African section declined while that of the creole increased. Although the slave population declined numerically between 1807 and 1834, this was due mainly to exports and not an unhealthy rate of natural increase. The Bahamas' slave population at emancipation was youthful, mainly creole, healthy and expanding.[22]

The Loyalist Revolution therefore introduced a slave population more likely to be creole and a population more likely to have an even sex-ratio. It followed then that there was more likelihood of stable family units and even the development of a monogamous slave family, which Herbert Gutman argued for among American slaves in his important *The Black Family in Slavery and Freedom*, 1750-1925 (New York 1976). Gutman's view was diametrically opposed to the traditional view that the slave family was unstable and that slaves had little family life, living in a cultural void.

The family patterns for which Gutman argued, probably continued in the Bahamas. Dr Barry Higman's novel argument for a common nuclear, two-headed household among slaves began much reinvestigation. Professor Michael Craton's study of twenty-six slave holdings in the Bahamas[23] and this author's analysis of the Farquharson Estate slaves over the Registration period, demonstrated the existence of monogamous unions among Bahamian slaves. The evidence seems to suggest strongly that the pattern was inherited from those slaves brought by the Loyalists.

Another important factor relating to slaves who were brought in by the Loyalists was that they were used to living in small units. The average size of a holding in Virginia and Maryland at the end of the eighteenth century was less than thirteen slaves. At the 1790 Census, the average slave holding in the principal plantation countries of Virginia and Maryland (where slave holdings were then the largest in the south) was only 8.5 and 13.[24]

Not all slaves in the south lived on large farms or were members of large work forces. Some were held as city slaves, hired out as craftsmen and domestics. Many therefore did not work on plantations, but belonged to small planters or yeomen, owning anything from one to a dozen slaves. Such slave holders were scattered throughout the south. Large plantations in fact were the exception rather than the rule. Half the slaves in the eighteenth century south lived on farms and not on plantations as defined by contemporaries, that is, in units of twenty or more. Generally speaking, the Loyalists who brought slaves had not owned large numbers of slaves. An exception was Denys Rolle who brought over one hundred slaves from East Florida to the Bahamas.

STUDY OF THREE GROUPS OF LOYALIST SLAVES

The Rolle Slaves[25]

Denys Rolle of Devonshire, England was a wealthy philanthropist and not a Loyalist in the strict sense. He had taken an assorted group of three hundred persons from the London slums and settled them on the eastern bank of the St Johns River. There he built a two-storeyed mansion and laid out a town behind it. At first it was called Charlotia after Queen Charlotte, the wife of George 111. Later it became known as Rollestown or Rolleston.

Rolle's venture was not successful; many of the original settlers who were white, fled, seeking an easier life. To some extent they were replaced by negro slaves. Some revival of the plantation occurred with the coming of the Loyalists. At the time of the evacuation of East Florida, Rolle had about one hundred and forty slaves. He transported them along with his livestock, dismantled houses and other possessions on the *Peace and Plenty*, (which is the name of a present-day hotel in George town) to Exuma Island in the Bahamas.

The first settlements were made on two tracts of land totalling about 2,000 acres granted by the Crown to Denys Rolle on Exuma. The original holdings were called Rolleville and Rolletown and their names remain to this day. Later the Rolle lands were increased to 5,000 acres by the purchase of two areas in the centre of Exuma. Rolle named the additional settlements Steventon, Ramsey and Mount Thompson.

Cotton plantations were set up but never flourished due to soil exhaustion and the attack of the chenille bug. Denys Rolle left the Bahamas to live in England, while his Exuma Estate was managed by an overseer, Thomas Thompson, resident in Exuma, and an attorney or agent, John C. Lees, who lived in Nassau. When he died in 1797, Denys Rolle's lands were inherited by his only son, John, an ardent follower of Pitt in the English House of Commons. John Rolle was raised to the peerage as Baron Rolle of Stevenstone in June 1796, taking the title of his uncle who had died without issue.

The Rolles purchased no more slaves on the general market after 1784. When the first triennial return of the Bahamian slaves was made in January 1822, Lord Rolle's holdings had grown to two hundred and fifty-four. By 1834, due to a high rate of

Rolle Town, Exuma

Rolleville, Exuma

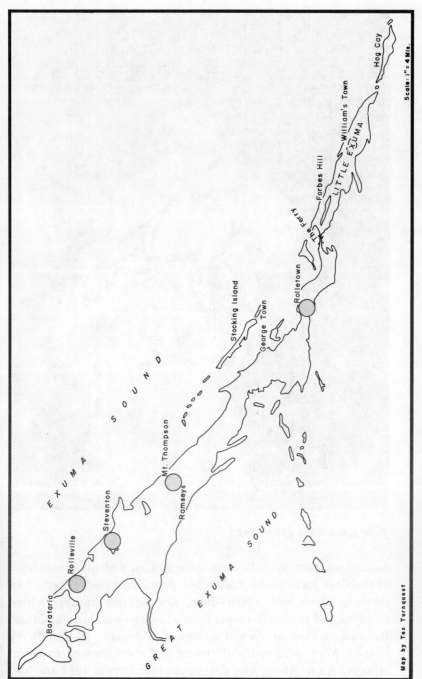

Exuma, showing the Rolle settlements between 1785 and 1834

Map by Tex Turquest

Scale:1"= 4 Mls.

John Lord Rolle 1750–1842

natural increase, a fairly constant sex-ratio, and the creolisation of the slave society, the Rolle slave population had increased to three hundred and seventy-four. Out of this number, three hundred and twenty-five were located at Exuma, thirty at Grand Bahama, eleven at New Providence and eight on the Berry Islands. Most were youthful creoles and there seemed to be no miscegenation. About fifty slaves were over forty in 1822 and had most probably been brought to Exuma in 1784. Most however, were under forty in 1822 and therefore were most likely to have been born in Exuma.

The Rolle slaves, both male and female, were mainly employed as field or agricultural workers. However, because of the failure of cotton, the plantation system had declined and their labour was less intensive than a comparable sugar plantation in Jamaica. Male slaves were also employed as mariners, either fishing and conching, or in droughing vessels, transporting goods between the Rolle plantations and, perhaps, Nassau. There were also nine male craftsmen, two plaitters, two jobbing carpenters, one mason, one apprenticed shipwright and one gardener. There were also seven drivers and two nurses among the male slave population. The range of possibilities was much more limited for females than males. The majority of females were employed in the field; a very small number were involved in domestic work and the minding of infants.

Between 1818 and 1828 Lord Rolle had spent over £5,000 to support his slaves at Exuma, while his return during those years was about £130 from cotton production. Like many Loyalists Rolle was forced to diversify; growing corn and peas, raking salt and raising cattle and sheep on his lands. Small wonder that he put in a request to the Colonial Office to move his slaves to Trinidad in 1828. It was Rolle's persistent attempts to move them that led to collective resistance among his slaves.

By 1822 the Rolle slaves lived in families, the predominant household being the nuclear-type family. Because of the decline of cotton, the slaves were left more and more to their own devices and seemingly had much freedom and mobility. They developed their own provision grounds, tended their animals, fished and gradually came to spend more time at their own affairs. It appeared from the records that they were strongly attached to their homes and their farm lands. By the 1830s they had probably become self-sufficient in food production.

Therefore when, in the face of severe losses, Rolle proposed to move some of his slaves to Trinidad in 1828, his plans filtered down to the slaves and caused much trouble. Sending his Attorney, Mr Lees, a Justice of the Peace and Member of the Legislative Council down to Exuma to ask the slaves if they would mind being moved to Trinidad, Rolle received a resounding no in answer. They refused to go to Trinidad, but agreed to be moved to another island in the Bahamas. However, when the time arrived for the transfer, Rolle's slaves refused and troops had to be called to force about twenty to be moved. Rolle's plan to move a further seventy-seven slaves in family groups from Exuma to Cat Island, where they were to be rented out to a Mr Thompson, also failed. When the slaves were informed, with only three days' notice, that they were to be moved, they objected. In spite of the fact that they were given three days to pick their crops and dispose of animals, they resisted. Under the leadership of Pompey, a 38-year-old black creole slave, forty-four of them including five men, eight women and their families, all creoles, disappeared into the woods for about five weeks after which they took Rolle's boat and set sail for Nassau.

Unfortunately for the runaways, they were captured in Nassau Harbour and put in the workhouse where they were severely flogged. On their return to Stevenston about two months later, their fellow slaves gave them a heroes' welcome and then promptly refused to work. The overseer, Mr Thompson, becoming alarmed, especially since he knew that several slaves had muskets, feared the outbreak of open rebellion. Governor Smyth, who had opposed the cruel treatment of the Rolle slaves in the Nassau workhouse, sent fifty regular soldiers to Stevenston. They met the slaves quiet but still refusing to work. When the soldiers searched the slave houses in the settlement they found twenty-five very indifferent muskets and a small amount of gunpowder. Taking all the Stevenston slaves prisoners and locking them up, the soldiers under Captain McPherson set off for Rolleville, five miles away, only to find on their arrival that Pompey had taken a short-cut along the beach and warned his fellow slaves who all hid in the bush.

A few more muskets were found in the huts of the Rolleville slaves, Pompey was caught, but it was not until he was whipped that the Rolle slaves agreed to go back to work. Even then, they refused to work more than half a day; insisting on working at their own business in the afternoon. This intransigent attitude continued and there was further trouble from the Rolle slaves in 1833 and 1834. Troops had to be sent to Exuma at least three times in the latter year.

The resistance among the Rolle slaves showed their determination not to be moved against their will. They wished to be free and had heard rumours that in fact they were. They aspired to be independent farmers and work for themselves. In fact they were attached to their homes, families and lands and were an example of what anthropologist Sidney Mintz and historian Douglas Hall have called proto-peasants. In other words, they desired to be left alone to work their own provision grounds using their own methods.

Pompey's revolt was merely one of the several that occurred in the Bahamas. Other miniature rebellions broke out in Eleuthera on the William Johnson Estate, at Cat Island on the Joseph Hunter Plantation and at Watlings or Farquharsons (see below). There was some trouble in the town of Nassau in 1832 reported in the *Bahamas Argus* which was anti-Governor Carmichael Smyth. On 12 and 13 January 1832, it stated: 'A number of men and women have paraded the streets of this Town (Nassau) armed with various weapons, threatening the lives of white inhabitants'. According to the report (printed on 14 January) two people were seriously maimed. However, the chief centres of revolt were on the Out Islands or in the rural areas rather than in the town where many slaves had gained quasi-independence or bought their freedom. The slaves on the Out Islands aspired towards complete freedom. It was not to their advantage to have quasi-freedom in the rural areas.

Legend has it that Lord Rolle granted his lands to be held in commonage to his former slaves. However, no deed has been found to support this belief, and his will, written three years after emancipation, directed his executors to sell his property in the Bahama Islands. Pompey's generation, as part of their resistance, probably claimed the land, became squatters and won it through their own independence. Some of the legal problems created by the squatters were resolved by the passage of the Commonage Act in April 1896. It seems that all of the Rolle slaves adopted the surname Rolle and therefore there are many Rolles in the modern Bahamas. Today, anyone with the surname Rolle, or with strong family relationships can build on the old Rolle property.

The Farquharson Slaves[26]

Charles Farquharson was a Loyalist of Scottish descent. He received an original Crown Grant of five hundred acres and

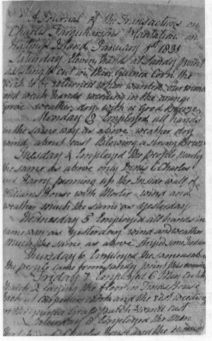

(left)   *From Farquharson's Journal (original) p.1*
(right) *From Farquharson's Journal (original) p.85*

settled at Prospect Hill on the east side of Watlings Island with the Creek to the east and the Great Lake to the west. Farquharson later obtained 1,400 additional acres from the Crown. On the north and south Farquharson was bounded by other estates but his was one of the largest on the island. Unlike Lord Rolle, Farquharson actually lived on his plantation and wrote a journal of the day-to-day happenings on the estate from 1 January 1831 to 31 December 1832. It was edited by the A. Deans Peggs Research Fund as *A Relic of Slavery* in 1957. Farquharson lived with his wife, two daughters, Christianna and Mary and one son James. Farquharson himself was a Justice of the Peace for the Island. The ruins of his modest plantation can still be seen today on San Salvador.

In 1822 during the first triennial registration of slaves, Farquharson owned thirty-five slaves comprising twenty females and fifteen males. The majority were creoles and there was one

(left)   *Ruins at Farquharson's plantation, San Salvador*
(right)   *Oven and fireplace at Farquharson's Estate, San Salvador*

Plantation ruins on the Farquharson Estate, San Salvador (the kitchen is on the left)

29

mulatto, probably fathered by James Farquharson. By emancipation year, due mainly to natural increase, the slaves had increased to fifty-two. Three Africans had died, and the one mulatto slave was freed in 1824. However, another mulatto was born between 1831 and 1834.

The Farquharson slaves were predominantly youthful and lived in families. The most common family household unit consisted of a man, his wife and their children or the nuclear family. There were also single slaves who had no family but lived alone or with friends. Some slaves had mates on other plantations. Diana, for example, was sent to the Dixon Estate 'to work and to be a wife for his Cuffey as it appears that she is already with child for Cuffey. . . .'[27]

It is apparent from Farquharson's Journal that the owner of the Estate and his slaves lived almost at subsistence level. Cotton was the chief commercial crop but only twelve bales were exported in two years. A variety of crops were grown: guinea corn, pigeon peas, Indian corn, fodder for cattle, red or cow peas, black-eye peas, yams, sweet potatoes, snap beans, castor oil and cabbage. These were mainly for consumption by the Farquharson family and their slaves. Stock such as sheep, pigs, steer, heifers and fowls were also raised. Some were exported as were a few tons of lignum vitae. The estate seemed to be self-sufficient. The sea yielded salt and fish and the woods, wattle and thatch for the houses of the slaves. Mules and horses were bred for use in transport.

Slaves were given a variety of jobs but were classified mainly as field workers, domestics and some as nurses who were left to mind infant slaves. Field slaves plaitted, weeded and harvested cotton and other crops. They also cut thatch, plastered houses, laid floors and did carpentry. Domestic slaves had to cook, clean house, sew, launder clothes and wait on table. Slaves also fished and raked salt.

The independence and close family and kinship ties of the Farquharson slaves was vividly demonstrated in March 1832 when a mutiny occurred at the plantation. The revolt erupted because James Farquharson, Charles' son, hit Isaac, one of the slaves, for mounting a mule on the wrong side, after having ordered him to do it correctly. Isaac's brother Alick took exception and came to his defence, asking James what right had he to beat Isaac so. James reacted strongly and began beating Alick who retaliated

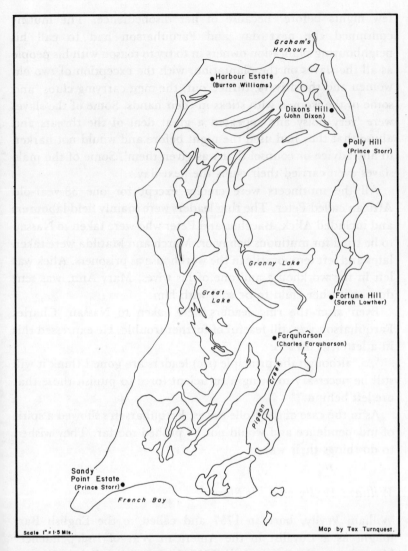

Scale 1" = 1·5 Mls.   Map by Tex Turnquest.

*San Salvador, showing the main settlements and their probable owners
or occupiers between 1783 and 1834*

until another slave Matilda stopped him. Alick said his intention
was to kill James. By this time, all fifty-two of the Farquharson
slaves had gathered and like so many furies were threatening
vegeance against James. Farquharson alluded to the real cause of
Alick's feelings. He attributed it to the fact that James had spoken
very sharply to Lisy, Alick's (Alexander's) wife, in the kitchen a

few nights before, because of her disobedience. The mutiny continued the next day and Farquharson had to call his neighbouring plantation owners in to try to reason with his people as all the slaves on the plantation, with the exception of two old women and the drivers, turned out, the men carrying clubs, and some of the women with sticks in their hands. Some of the slaves were 'very noisy and repeated a great deal of the threats and abuse that they had used the night before and would not harken to any advice or counsel that was given them'. Some of the male slaves even carried their clubs the next day.

All the mutineers were creoles except for one 38-year-old African called Peter. The ring leaders were mainly field labourers and included Alick, Bacchus and Peter who were taken to Nassau to be tried for mutinous behavior. March and Matilda were taken later and left temporarily in the workhouse as prisoners. Alick was left in the workhouse and one of his wives, Mary Ann, was sent down with her child to be sold with him.

Even after the ring leaders were taken to Nassau, Charles Farquharson was still fearful of further trouble. He expressed this in a letter to his son:

'. . . although the principle (sic) leaders are gone I think it will still be necessary to bring a sufficient force to punish those that are left behind.'[28]

As in the case of the Rolle slaves, Farquharson's showed a spirit of independence and would not be pushed too far. They wished to do things their way.

William Wylly and his Slaves[29]

William Wylly, born in 1757 and called to the English Bar, fought as a Loyalist in the American War of Independence. Migrating to the Bahamas in 1787, he became Solicitor General in the same year. In 1797, he was promoted to Attorney General of the Bahamas. From his arrival in the Bahamas until his death in 1828, Wylly played an important part in Bahamian affairs.

A critic of the controversial Governor, Lord Dunmore, Wylly is best known for the crisis which erupted in 1816. Himself a slave-owner, Wylly, presiding over the Court of the Vice Admiralty, challenged the authority of master over slaves, a decision that caused a serious rift between the executive and legislature and delayed the passing of the Registration Act until 1821. The whole incident blew up into what has popularly become known as the Wylly Affair, over the sentence given by Wylly to General Robert Cunningham's (a Loyalist) slave.

The House of Assembly violently objected to Wylly's action which had been based on an Imperial Statute of 1806. Infuriated, the Assembly appointed a committee to investigate the Wylly case, and Wylly summoned to appear before the committee, refused. The House retaliated, sending the Provost Marshall, William Chrisholm, on the night of 22 January 1817 to the Wylly Estate at Clifton, to arrest him. Wylly resisted arrest by arming his negroes with muskets and bayonets and posting them at his gates. Later arrested and imprisoned, Wylly within two hours had obtained a writ of *habeas corpus*, was given bail and freed. The House of Assembly was furious and the Governor had to dissolve the House in January 1817. The new House held Wylly in no less contempt and censured him. A very unruly House, which itself was censured by the Imperial Government, had to be dissolved again. It was not until late in 1820 that the Assembly passed what is known as the Healing Act and finally in April 1821, a Triennial Registration Act.

By 1818 William Wylly had sixty-seven slaves on three plantations at the western end of New Providence. The main estate was Clifton, the largest, where provisions were raised by and for the slaves. The other two were Tusculum between the present-day Orange Hill and Gambier Village, and Waterloo just west of Lightbourn Creek. The latter two estates had been turned over to stock-raising. The slaves at Clifton were allowed to work on their own provision grounds for two or three days a week and separate pastures were allotted for their hogs. Slaves were also allowed to take their pigs, poultry and produce to market on Saturdays. Wylly, however, supplemented their provisions.

From the lists of the Registers of Slaves 1821 and the Governor's Correspondence[30] there is strong evidence that the Wylly slaves, like those of Rolle and Farquharson, lived in families, mainly in nuclear-type households. In fact Wylly was concerned that his slaves should marry and rewarded slaves who took their first wife to a 'well built stone house' with a 'sow pig' and a 'pair of dung hill fowls'. Slaves were to be punished for committing adultery. They lost their hogs, poultry and other moveable effects and suffered the humiliating experience of having their heads shaved and wearing sack cloth for six months. Additionally, they were confined to the plantation.

Wylly also made sure his slaves received religious instruction. The distance of about seventeen miles from Nassau to Clifton deterred the Anglican clergyman, and Wylly requested help in 1813 from the Methodist Mission, which complied. In fact Wylly set aside about twenty pounds to pay a minister to visit the slaves at Clifton at least four times a year. In addition Wylly's slaves attended a chapel on the Estate every Sunday to hear prayers read to them by the driver. The driver and the overseer, James Rutherford, a free black man, were obviously literate. In fact Wylly encouraged his slaves to learn to read and write. Prayer and spelling books were supplied and drivers who were able, were paid for teaching the other slaves to read.

Slaves on Wylly's estate also seemed to have some leisure time and freedom of movement. The drivers and principal herdsman of Tusculum were very privileged, having horses for transportation. The ordinary slaves were allowed to go to town on Saturdays to sell produce in the Nassau market. At Christmas they were given three days off and allowed to go where they pleased. They were also given a half-day on Saturdays.

Compared to other British West Indian slaves, they were fairly well clothed, being given two suits of osnaburgs and a woollen suit each year. They were also allowed a blanket once in three years. Their punishment was controlled, the drivers not being allowed to give more than twelve stripes except with Wylly's permission. However, runaways were quite severely·punished.

All slaves were cared for in a special hospital and mothers had access to a nursery for their children during the day while they worked. Nursing mothers worked near the nursery. All in all, Wylly seemed to have been a benevolent master to his slaves.

Evidence is scant about exactly how slaves thought and what they did in their leisure time. Very few slaves could read and write and so far no writings of Bahamian slaves have come to light. We must therefore rely on European sources which tell only half the story. However, it is fortunate that records such as the *Relic of Slavery* and Wylly's Regulations and the slave Registers have survived. The descendants of the slaves of the Loyalists influenced Bahamian history. The original slaves brought were almost immediately utilised in cotton-growing. When the plantations failed, they helped their masters in subsistence farming, as domestics, salt-rakers and mariners. The life-style they developed in the Bahamian environment and their struggle to survive against almost insurmountable odds, have helped to shape the resilient Bahamian character.

[3]

Economic Influence
of the Loyalists

HE STATE OF THE ECONOMY OF THE Bahama Islands just prior to the coming of the Loyalists was weak. In 1773 there was general economic distress with little revenue and an economy based mainly on wrecking and turtling. During the American War of Independence the Bahamas prospered. It was used in 1779 as a trading base by American rebels.[31] Trade ensued between the rebels and some inhabitants of the Bahamas. Rich cargoes were apparently discharged close to Fort Montagu.

Ironically, the Bahamas also benefited tremendously as a privateering base, but with many rebel ships being captured by the British and brought to the Bahamas between 1779 and 1780[32] and condemned in the Court of Vice Admiralty at New Providence in 1782, supplies dwindled dramatically. Following Rodney's victory at the Battle of the Saints in that year, Britain controlled the Caribbean sea.

The coming of the Loyalists brought economic growth to the Bahamas, at least temporarily. Besides introducing the growing of cotton, the Loyalists brought new wealth witnessed in the new buildings and churches. The Government also purchased the land at Mount Fitzwilliam where the official residence of the Governor was soon to be built, and showed a responsive attitude towards the poor in the community.

Initially the Loyalists grew Persian cotton which many of them had grown in Georgia. Then they experimented with Anguilla, a longer staple cotton. The latter grew all year round and became as large as small trees unless pruned.[33]

Because of the paper money problems being experienced in the fledgling United States, inflation was imported causing spiralling prices for food and other goods, especially between 1785 and 1788.[34] However, the economy expanded dramatically between 1785 and 1788 due to cotton exports. After a set back caused by the attacks of the chenille and red bugs, there was also economic growth due to cotton exports in the 1790s and early 1800s.

A sign of better economic conditions was witnessed by the fact that Governor Dunmore's salary was increased three times between 1787 and 1794.[35] The economy of the Bahamas as a whole was affected.

The Planter Loyalists who went south and those who settled in the north both had an economic impact on the Bahamas. Loyalist shipbuilders who included John Russell, William Begbie and Daniel Manson introduced a prosperous trade, bringing much foreign capital into the Bahamas. With the influx of professionals, such as doctors, lawyers, accountants and merchants, commercial life was given a further boost. Stores blossomed over Nassau. Some companies which had successfully traded with the Indians in the Southern States moved their head-quarters to Nassau. One firm was Panton, Leslie and Company. There were others, including Miller, Bonnamy and Company, but it was the Planter Loyalists who mainly went south, who tried, albeit unsuccessfully to revolutionise the Bahamian way of life.

COTTON PRODUCTION

Those Loyalists who went south mainly to Watlings, Exuma, San Salvador (that is, Cat Island), Long Island and Crooked and Acklins Island between 1784 and 1785 to set up cotton plantations, had great hopes of prosperity. By November 1785, over two thousand acres of cotton were under cultivation in the Bahamas. For a few years it looked as though the Loyalists' hopes would be fulfilled.

In 1785 the Bahamas produced 124 tons of cotton from 2,476 acres. Production for the years 1786 and 1787 was 150 tons and

Believed to be the son of Joseph Eve

219 tons from 3,050 and 4,500 acres respectively. Expectations for 1788 were high, but alas, only 112 tons were produced, the remaining 282 tons having been almost completely destroyed by the chenille and red bug. Other crops such as guinea and Indian corn were also hit.

Cotton-growing and exports of the crop however, continued throughout the 1790s and early 1800s. In fact export figures for the early 1790s were higher than those for 1786 and 1787, and those for 1809 and 1810 even higher. It was reported that 4,160 bales were exported from the ports of Nassau and Exuma in 1790 weighing 442 tons.[36] There was an increase in the next year when 5,163 bales were exported weighing 492 tons.[37]

Cotton gin invented by Joseph Eve

Perhaps the invention of Joseph Eve's cotton gin in 1793 boosted cotton production. Eve, probably born in South Carolina, lived in Pennsylvania at the time of the American Revolution and was thought to have been a Quaker. His machine was turned by the wind, horse or cattle, or water power if there was an inlet. The machine was able to gin more than 360 pounds of cotton in one day and the United States became a major producer of cotton after its invention. Apparently the machine was efficient. Charles Dames, a fellow Loyalist planter, wrote in May, 1794:

'Dear Sir ... this is now the third year in which I have enjoyed the benefit of your most useful machine for cleaning cotton. The favourable opinion I conceived of it on the first trial, must in your recollection .... . Preparing our cotton for market was formerly considered most tedious, troublesome and laborious part of the Agricultural process in this country. To you we are indebted for its having been pleasant, easy and expeditious.'[38]

However, by 1800, most of the cotton planters were facing ruin and the Bahamian Government's questionnaire in that year, sent to twenty-five leading cotton growers, revealed that failure was principally due to the exhausted state of the soil, the inexperience of the planters and consequent injudicious planting, the attack of the chenille and red bug, bad management and climate. The soil was thin and the slash and burn method usually employed to clear the fields eventually led to soil exhaustion. Manure was difficult to obtain as many planters had no cattle.

To add to the technical difficulties, the chenille had attacked the cotton crops of the Bahamas again in 1794. By 1803, McKinnen, a British traveller through the West Indies calculated that three-quarters of the crops of cotton had been destroyed from the attack of the chenille in 1788 and 1794.[39] He added that the red bug had also damaged the cotton crops in places. An Act had to be passed in 1798 to prevent or control cotton bugs.

Some cotton plantations at the time of McKinnen's visit were still very active. Caicos Island, then a part of the Bahamas, had the best soil and cotton was still a staple in 1803. Crooked Island however, where many Loyalists had settled and established about forty plantations with about one thousand slaves, had suffered decline. McKinnen stated:

'I beheld some extensive fields originally planted with cotton, but which from the failure of crops were now abandoned, and had become covered with a luxuriant growth of indigenous shrubs and plants . . .'[40]

'I found the plantations on Crooked Island for the most part deserted; and the proprietors who I visited were generally in a state of despondence, in an agricultural point of view as to the future.'[41]

Exactly when the serious decline of cotton began is not known. Cotton exports to the United States between 1794 and 1805 seriously diminished and it was evident that cotton as a staple was a failure, although 1809 and 1810 were good years, yielding 509 and 602 tons respectively. By 1832, however, cotton produced in the Bahamas totalled 42 tons.[42] No evidence could be found for cotton exports between 1810 and 1832 and it is therefore difficult to ascertain when the real decline of cotton finally set in.

Because many of the Loyalists had invested all that they had in their plantations, they were tied to them. A good number tried to sell them in the late eighteenth and early nineteenth centuries. When that failed, the planters were forced to resort to the old subsistence crops such as guinea corn and yams and took to the seafaring life of the older inhabitants. Some cotton was still grown in, the 1860s according to Governor Rawson's *Report on the Bahamas' Hurricane of October 1866*. Many also turned to salt-raking.

SALT PRODUCTION

The Bahamas were endowed with natural salt ponds or shallow lagoons where sea water evaporated rapidly and formed chunks of salt crystals. Salt had been exported from the Bahamas from at least the beginning of the eighteenth century. Turks Island which was incorporated into the Bahamas' Government in 1799 was especially renowned for salt from an early period. Small ponds had also been operated by the older inhabitants at Rose Island, near New Providence where the remains of the salt ponds can still be seen, and at Eleuthera.

Salt pans in Inagua

41

Peters maintained that the Loyalists did not move to Turks Island but raked salt in the plantation Islands. This was certainly true in Exuma (salinas are most evident near the old Hermitage Estate in Williams Town, Little Exuma, owned during slavery times by the Kelsalls), Long Island, Acklins and Long Cay. However, perhaps one of the most productive salt ponds at that time was Duncan's Town, Ragged Island. There, the pond was built by two Loyalists, Duncan and Archibald Taylor. Many of the Loyalists occupied their slaves in the arduous tasks of salt-raking towards the end of April after the cotton had been picked in the spring.

Slaves employed in salt production perhaps had the hardest tasks and suffered more illness than other slaves. Salt-raking was rough and taxing labour. Slaves had to wait for the weather to crystallise the salt in salinas. The solid crystals then had to be broken and raked a shore. However, to facilitate the process, salt pans were made. As the salt was taken out, it was replenished with brine from the pond. Once it was raked into piles, it had to be packed and transported to a port which was difficult with only animal and human transportation. Conditions were harsh as the bright sunlight, reflecting against the white salt affected the eyes.

Salt no doubt played an important part in the economy of the Bahamas. From 1789 salt-raking was regulated by law and salt commissioners were appointed by the Governor to serve each island or group of islands where there were salt ponds. An export duty levied by the Colonial Government helped to raise a sizeable revenue for the small colony.

STOCK-RAISING

With the decline of cotton, stock-raising was also attempted by the Loyalists. Sheep and goats thrived better than cattle since they could survive on scrub pasturage with little water. West Indian sheep did well at Exuma. A plantation journal kept on that island lists the extraordinary increase of seven goats purchased in May 1786 to one hundred and fifty-one in 1789.[43] Burton Williams and Charles Farquharson, both of Watlings had raised cattle and sheep in the Bahamas. Farquharson shipped four heads of cattle, sixteen sheep and five pigs to Nassau in May 1831.[44]

By 1832, stock-raising was indeed important to nearly all the islands, especially New Providence, Rum Cay, Long Island, Watlings Island, Exuma and Cat Island. Long Island was the largest producer of stock. More horses and cattle were produced on Long Island than on any other island. It also produced the largest amount of sheep, goats and swine. Cat Island produced the second largest amount of sheep and goats and the second largest amount of cattle. New Providence produced the second largest number of horses next to Long Island.

In spite of the decline of cotton, the Loyalist impact on the economy was significant. Although some slaves, such as those belonging to James Moss of Crooked Island and Acklins and those of Burton Williams of Watlings Island were transferred to other West Indian Islands, most of them remained in the Bahamas. Many stayed on the lands of their former owners as tenants and some formed villages, others became squatters. Their attachment to the land, their subsistence farming and the methods employed are deeply ingrained in Bahamian Out (Family) Island life.

In modern times there has been a tremendous urban drift from the Out Islands to Nassau. Some Bahamians migrated in the late nineteenth and early twentieth century to Florida, Key West in Florida and other parts of America. However, there remains today a substantial number of descendants of the Loyalists' slaves who have managed to survive for generations through their farming. Cotton may have failed, but the alternative occupations such as subsistence farming, salt production and stock-rearing are still viable and are important occupations in contemporary Bahamian life.

Social Effects
& Political Influence

OCIALLY THE LOYALISTS GREATLY influenced Bahamian life. They introduced their own concept of plantation life and that of the relationship of master and slave. The increase in the slave population made for more stringent controls by the ruling class. Besides influencing the class structure, the Loyalists also contributed to the cultural life of the Bahamas. The creole society which evolved saw strong influences from both Europe and Africa. The growth of the town was positively affected and there was a change in the style of architecture, both private and public. In fact the whole tone of Bahamian society was affected. Politically, the Loyalist era saw many conflicts between the old and new inhabitants. The latter eventually took the upper hand.

SOCIAL STRUCTURE

West Indian Colonial Society was based on a hierarchical structure reflecting colour and class. During slavery the minority and influential white ruling class, usually supported by the Imperial Government, headed the social pyramid. At the lowest level were the slaves and in between were the free coloureds who were separated from both the black slaves and the white élite. These colour and class barriers in the Bahamas were intensified after the coming of the Loyalists. Race and economics were no doubt linked.

Because of the increased numbers of black slaves, the Loyalists passed harsh vagrancy laws and regulations to separate the races on New Providence in the early 1790s. Before that time housing for whites and blacks was intermixed throughout Nassau, some slaves living either within or behind the larger homes of their owners. Freed blacks resided in the town. But with a trebled black population after 1785, stricter control for segregating them from the whites in the town was enforced. An act for Regulating the Police of the Town of Nassau and Surburbs passed between 1795 and 1798, demanded that all people of colour be off the streets of the town of Nassau after 9.00 p.m. when the Town Bell rang.

Two areas which were set aside for the blacks during slavery were the present-day Grant's Town, a wooded, swampy area which was surveyed in the 1820s under the administration of Governor Grant, and Delancey Town, named after a slave owner and Chief Justice of the Bahamas, Stephen Delancey. Although

A native African hut

these were settled, mainly by Liberated Africans who had been captured by the Royal Navy and freed in the Bahamas mainly on New Providence, it is conjectured that many freed slaves also settled in these areas. Another black settlement near Nassau which developed in the 1840s was Bain Town adjacent to Grant's Town. Liberated Africans were also settled at Carmichael, Adelaide and Fox Hill or Sandilands Village.

Another act passed shortly after the arrival of the Loyalists was one to ascertain who shall not be deemed Mulattoes. Any one above three degrees removed in a lineal descent from the Negro ancestor was to be considered white.

While Nassau developed into a quaint and architecturally attractive colonial town reserved for the white élite, Grant's Town, over-the-hill from Nassau had always much poorer and more humble buildings and its settlers lacked the necessary capital to develop it properly. It was allowed to grow without supervision. In its early years it boasted a market and had many fruit and other trees. Vegetables were also grown there. A slow decline in the area set in after the mid-nineteenth century when some families moved into the surburbs, and during the 1880s

A scene in Grant's Town, c.1891

46

View of a part of Grant's Town, c.1880

Street scene in Grant's Town

Early morning in Nassau market

many emigrated abroad. As Doran and Landis, two geographers from Radford University, Virginia[45] argued, the over-the-hill area changed from owner-occupier to tenant occupied. This had a profound effect on the area which came to be looked down upon as an enclave for social inferiors.[46] The over-the-hill area in the nineteenth century was occupied mainly by poor blacks who usually sought unskilled employment in Nassau.

ARCHITECTURAL CHANGES[47]

Nassau

In striking contrast to over-the-hill, Nassau was transformed by the Loyalists. Besides important architectural changes, streets were cleaned, repaired and new ones built. Docks and wharves were improved. New regulations, for example, one prohibiting thatched roofs in Nassau in order to protect home owners against fire, were passed. There was an improvement to cemeteries which were to be enclosed and a regulation passed that graves must be at least four feet deep.

Architecturally, the Loyalists had a tremendous impact on the town. Much of the architectural style of the Southern States was transported to Nassau. The American colonists before the Revolutionary War had already established their own variations of Georgian architecture. Most of the material used in the early southern colonial towns was wood. Stone was rarely used. However, in Nassau, both were employed because they were readily available. In 1783, the houses in Nassau were mainly of wood and lightly built, but in the early 1800s Daniel McKinnen, a traveller, found that many houses were built of stone from local quarries, such as the one which was at the southern end of Elizabeth Avenue, the present site of the Queen's Staircase.

The Loyalists patterned their houses mainly on the Georgian style, but adapted them to meet the Bahamian climate and economic conditions. Most of the houses were similar in design, consisting basically of a simple rectangular plan, two to three storeys in height, usually with an attic. The ground floor was used as a basement to house storerooms and the servants' quarters. The main rooms were at first floor level. Kitchens were usually built away from the main house so as to avoid cooking smells and heat there. It was in fact a precaution against fire.

Another characteristic aspect of the architecture of Nassau was the use of quoins. Many Loyalist buildings also incorporated large rectangular blocks of local stone. Some homes also boasted delicately designed hard wood railings in a variety of patterns. Some houses had two-storeyed timber verandahs. High peaked roofs, dormer windows, brackets and lattice work, were also characteristic of this period. The shipbuilding industry, active in Nassau in the late eighteenth and early nineteenth centuries, was reflected in the use of peculiar features like wooden knees or brackets which still support the balconies of Balcony House in Market Street north.

Public Buildings
Not only did the Loyalists influence private architecture in the town, its suburbs and on the Out Islands (see below), they also greatly influenced public construction. Lord Dunmore who, although haughty and disliked by the inhabitants of Nassau, especially the Loyalists, left a lasting legacy on the architecture of the town. His mania for building resulted in the construction of Forts Charlotte and Fincastle, and batteries at Winton, Hog Island and Potter's Cay. He also built Dunmore House, popularly known

Fort Charlotte

Dunmore House

The Hermitage

Dunmore Town, Harbour Island

in modern times as the Priory, on West Street. For his private enjoyment he built two summer residences, the Hermitage on East Bay Street between 1787 and 1796, and then considered in the far east, and a house, now demolished, on Harbour Island, in Dunmore Town, which he laid out.

The Public Buildings, c.1812

Nassau Public Library c.1874

In 1783, the public buildings had comprised a church, a gaol and an assembly house. Within thirty years there were at least five substantial notable new buildings, including the Public Buildings, the jail, Government House and two churches, all with a decidely Loyalist architectural influence.[48]

The Public Buildings today

Nassau Public Library today

Completed between 1812 and 1816, the Public Buildings were based on Governor Tryon's Palace in New Bern, the ancient capital of North Carolina. They are situated at the northern end of Parliament Street and faced on to Bay Street. At the time of their construction, Rawson Square did not exist and the buildings were only separated from the harbour by Bay Street.

Nassau Public Library, built between 1798 and 1799 was said to have been inspired by the old Powder Magazine in Williamsburg, Virginia. Its octagonal shape is unusual and it served originally as a prison.

The building of the modern Government House seemed to have been inspired by Loyalists as well. Situated on top of the hill known as Mount Fitzwilliam, it was completed in about 1806 and occupied shortly afterwards by Governor Cameron and his family.

Two Nassau churches, one Anglican, the other Presbyterian, were also Loyalist inspired. St Matthew's, built between 1800 and 1802 to accommodate Anglicans in the eastern district of Nassau, was designed and built by Loyalist Joseph Eve, and is the oldest

St Matthew's Church, c.1844

extant church building in Nassau. In 1823 it was considered to be at the eastern extremity of the town. It has recently been restored and its tower and spire are today important landmarks in the city of Nassau.

St Matthew's Church today

Another Loyalist, Michael Malcolm was instrumental in getting the Kirk built. Its construction resulted from a plea to the St Andrew's Society, founded in 1798 in Nassau. The corner-stone of St Andrew's Presbyterian Church was laid in August 1810. Over the years it has undergone much renovation, but its basic Loyalist construction is still in evidence.

St Andrew's Kirk

The advent of the Loyalists, who passed regulations including those for the prevention of fires, animals wandering at large and the enclosure of cemeteries, changed the appearance of the town. The shabby little port was transformed 'into a town as well built as any in the West Indies'.

Out (Family) Islands

On the Out or Family Islands as they are now called, Loyalists built plantation buildings of stone using wood only for the roof and frames of windows. Plantations usually comprised a main house, a separate kitchen with a fireplace and chimney, perhaps a bakery, basic stables and slave quarters. These were modest plantations by comparison to those on the sugar colonies further south, and their remains can be seen at San Salvador (Farquharson's, Sandy Point and Fortune Hill), Long Island (Grey's and Dunmore's), Crooked Island (Hope House and Marine Farm), Cat Island (Deveaux House) and Exuma (the Hermitage at William's Town, Little Exuma).

Slave houses, usually built of stones or wattle and daub made of

(left)   *Ruins of Great House, Sandy Point, San Salvador*
(right)   *Ruins of the fireplace, Sandy Point, San Salvador*

sand and lime, were about fifteen to twenty feet by fourteen feet wide comprising one or two rooms. The roofs were thatched. Slave quarters were usually quite a distance from the Master's house. The slave houses at Farquharson's had gardens and were much more substantial than those at the Sandy Point Estate. In Nassau some remains can still be found of Wylly's Clifton Estate which once boasted large gates, a wide carriage drive leading to a three-storeyed house planned in the English style. It also had a coach-house and stables for several carriage horses and substantial slave quarters.

Remembering that most of the Out Islands were uninhabited or scantily inhabited in 1784, the Loyalists made a profound impact on the Out Islands. Many of the plantation buildings were occupied by former slaves long after emancipation.

OTHER CULTURAL INFLUENCES
European

Besides influencing the architecture of Nassau, its surburbs and the Out Islands, the Loyalists made a big impact on New Providence life. Record-keeping was improved. The books in the Registry were much better kept. Loyalists, Adam Chrystie and his assistant, James Armbrister took over. A lending library started and dramatic entertainment began. The British legal system which still survives today, was reinforced.

The first Bahamian newspaper, the *Bahama Gazette* was published for the first time on 7 August 1784 by John Wells, a Loyalist from Charleston, South Carolina. Wells had operated a paper in East Florida before migrating with his press to Nassau. Besides the Bahamas, Wells' newspaper was circulated in Charleston, Savannah and Bermuda. The *Bahama Gazette*'s motto, 'Nullius Addictus Jurare in Verba Magistri' (not bound in loyalty to any masters) is still used by the evening paper, *The Tribune*, today. John Wells also opened a book and stationery store, the only one in Nassau and published various items including the *Bahamas Almanac*. Two other Loyalist printers functioned for a while. Joseph Eve was a printer to the House of Assembly for a time, and Alexander Cameron a Virginian Loyalist founded a second, largely unknown Nassau newspaper, *The Lucayan Royal Herald*. It is interesting to note that a book of poems called *The Vision and Other Poems* was published by a Bahamian man of Colour in 1834, in London.

Religious and educational life was also strengthened during the late eighteenth century. By an Act of 1795 six parishes were created which included St Patrick's, Eleuthera; Saint Salvador, Cat Island; St Andrew, Exuma; St Paul's, Long Island; St David, Crooked Island; and St George's, Turks and Caicos Island. Christ Church, New Providence and St John's, Harbour Island, already existed. A new school Act was also passed in 1795 placing all schools under a central authority.

The slaves of the Loyalists also greatly influenced religious and social life.

African

The consensus among most American scholars of slavery is that slaves had a life independent from that of their masters. They kept alive many of their African customs diluted by their new environment and tribal dispersal. Slaves of the Loyalists brought their beliefs and practices with them from America. Much of their folklore, although shaped by the local environment, was passed on from generation to generation and still affects Bahamian culture today. Especially significant are the use of bush or herb medicine, the practice of Junkanoo, the Baptist religion, story-telling, music and dance, obeah and food and games.

Bush Medicine

The origin of the use of bush medicine in the Bahamas is obscure. However, as Mrs Leslie Higgs, a Bahamian authority on bush medicine states:

'For generations, people living in remote Bahamian Settlements have looked to nature's own apothecary to succour their ills'.[49]

During slavery there were physicians but some were of dubious reputation and methods and most lived in Nassau. The Out Islands were only occasionally visited by doctors. It seems that slaves took care of themselves using home methods. It can be conjectured that slaves used bush medicine still commonly used in the Bahamas today. Catnip, used as an appetiser, a health drink in pregnancy and a treatment for worms and colds, and sage bush, used to relieve itching of the skin, both grew on the Farquharson Estate near the slave quarters during slavery days. McKinnen in 1803 spoke of 'curious medicinal plants native to Crooked Island'. He actually stated that milk wood was good for curing worms. Perhaps the most popular bush medicine used in modern times for colds and fever is cerasee.

Junkanoo

It is almost certain that the modern Junkanoo festival was brought over by African slaves. Similar customs survived in Georgia, Jamaica and Bermuda.

There is much evidence that some type of dance was held at Christmas by the slaves or on the day after Christmas. Charles Farquharson wrote on 26 December 1832:

'Some of our people gone abroad to see some of their friends and some at home amusing themselves in their own way through the day, but all of them at home in the evening and had a grand dance and keep it up until near day light.'[50]

Dowson, a Methodist missionary who served in the West Indies between 1810 and 1817, on arriving at Turks Island (then one of the Bahamas) on Christmas Day, observed:

'I never before witnessed such a Christmas Day; the negroes have been beating their tambourines and dancing the whole day and now between eight and nine o'clock they are pursuing their sport as hotly as ever ...'[51]

This dance is almost certainly what we now celebrate as Junkanoo on Boxing Day and New Year's Day between 3.00 a.m. and 9.00 a.m. in the morning. Junkanoo is essentially a West African festival, although there are many theories as to its origin. By 1801, however, John Canoe was a fixture in the Bahamas. Today it has become almost an institution and is the soul of the Bahamian. Instruments used in the festivities and the modern day parade are cowbells, goatskin drums and whistles. The rushers thus make their own music.

Religion

The slaves had religious customs different to those of their white masters. Their music and their form of worship was alien to that of the whites. The slaves identified with the early Baptists and

Junkanoo in the 1930s

Junkanoo, 1979

Methodist missionaries who were originally black. After 1800 the leadership of the Methodist Church, however, was white. It was the Baptists who gained and kept the most black converts.

In fact many of the slaves and freed slaves from Georgia and South Carolina who came with the Loyalists had already been converted to the Methodist and Baptist faiths in America.[52]

Joseph Paul a freed slave was the first Methodist in the Bahamas. He arrived in Abaco with the Loyalists from North America probably in 1783. It is believed that he moved to Nassau between 1786 and 1794 where he began making converts and built a small wooden chapel on the corner of Augusta and Heath Field Streets. His early requests for help from the American Methodists were not very successful. In fact they were disruptive, splitting Paul's Society with the larger part being led by Anthony Wallace and his wife who were also free Negroes. In 1799 the Methodist Missionary Society in England sent William Turton, the mulatto son of a Barbadian planter, to the Bahamas. Turton associated himself with the Wallace faction and Paul's congregation and the original chapel passed out of Methodist hands.

The first white person was converted in 1803 and became Turton's wife. By 1806 a quarter of the Methodists in the Bahamas were white. The Police Act of 1816 which prohibited the holding of sectarian religious services between 6.00 a.m. and 6.00 p.m. probably did much to increase white Methodist membership. By the time of Emancipation, more than half the Bahamian Methodist members were white.

George Liele, a slave who had founded the first black Baptist Church in Savannah, finally obtained his freedom and later formed the first Baptist Church in Jamaica. Brother Amos, on the other hand, came to the Bahamas.

Evidence is scanty for the exact date that Amos arrived in New Providence. However, by 1791 his church was reportedly three hundred strong. Another early black Baptist in the Bahamas was Sambo Scriven, a runaway slave who was known among the Bahamas blacks as a Baptist preacher. Sambo Scriven, obtaining his freedom in 1790, was pastor of the Society of Anabaptists who in 1801 purchased the land on which the present Bethel Baptist Church stands. About this time, Prince Williams was made assistant pastor. He later became pastor after Sambo Scriven's

Early Bethel Baptist Church

death in 1822. The Baptists then met at Bethel Baptist Chapel, later splitting with members of Prince Williams' congregation and forming the St John's Native Baptist Church in March 1832.

The Baptist Church quickly gained converts. Religious worship was the only activity where slaves were allowed to congregate in large numbers and that was at times curtailed by law. While the established Anglican Church took little interest in the slaves, segregating them in cramped quarters, the Baptists, with their stress on freedom, their rousing music, emotional sermons, and their lively singing, hand-clapping and spirit possession, appealed to the Bahamian slaves and freed blacks. Customs such as the holding of wakes brought communities together. Clement Bethel believes that much of the music sung by slaves and their descendants was derived from the ante-bellum slave songs on the American mainland.[53]

Slaves and freed blacks could identify with the black leadership of the Baptist mission which was much more active among the ordinary people than the Established Church. The Baptists moreover trained black Bahamians early in pastoral duties and leadership positions. Today the Baptist Church is the largest denomination in the Bahamas.

Story-Telling, Music and Dance
Slaves gathered after work in their own quarters and made their own recreation. They sang, danced, talked and told stories. The habits, customs and way of life of the slaves in the Bahamas was

64

profoundly affected by the coming of the slaves of the Loyalists.

American slaves brought their own folklore. Story-telling which was passed down from generation to generation often concerned animals who experienced thrilling adventures and included the B'Booky and B'Rabby stories of American Negro-lore.

As Clement Bethel has demonstrated in his study of Bahamian music, the slaves enjoyed both religious and secular music. The latter, with a strong emphasis on drumming and dancing, was undoubtedly of African origin. The ring dance was perhaps the most popular form held to the accompaniment of the goatskin drum and there were three distinct types — the *Fire Dance*, the *Jumping Dance* and the *Ring Play*. Other dances such as the set dances, generally known as *Quadrilles* were of mixed African and European tradition.

Obeah

Obeah is not unique to the Bahamas. It is a West Indian phenomenon, although it is called by different names. A combination of superstitions, medicine and worship, it is most certainly of African origin. Wherever African slaves settled, African religious beliefs, healings superstitions still survive. Dr Timothy McCartney explored the subject in *Ten, Ten the Bible Ten: Obeah in the Bahamas*, Nassau, 1976. He sees Bahamian obeah as the phenomenon of the supernatural rendering good or evil. He stated that it can cause illnesses and can cure them. It can also cause death. He argued for a spiritualism surrounded with superstition.

Although no written evidence has come to light of slaves practising obeah, the fact that tales have been passed on such as the *Sammy Swain Legend* from Cat Island, (which was popularised in opera form by Clement Bethel in the late 1960s), shows that it probably existed in slavery times. Obeah and the use of bush medicine are related and as discussed already, we know that slaves grew and used bush medicine. Undoubtedly the slaves of the Loyalists brought some Vodoo or Obeah from the American Colonies, but it was the Liberated Africans who probably reinforced the obeah beliefs.

Food and Games

Slaves coming with the Loyalists no doubt influenced Bahamian cooking. Their style certainly survived into the early twentieth century. As H. M. Bell illustrated:

'Slaves cooked outside the kitchen on open fire. Three stones held their pots . . .'[54]

Slaves also cooked in a fireplace in the kitchen off the main house of the plantation. They also seemed to have had fireplaces built into their own houses. Some African dishes which are still remembered and cooked by some are accara, foo-foo, agedi and my-my.

Warri was an African game, originally played mainly by women. Today it is largely a pastime of men from over-the-hill. Warri is played on a board, usually by two persons and the object of the game is to win the majority of the forty-eight large seeds or marbles which are moved mathematically from well to well.

Bahamian creole culture has definitely been influenced by the slaves of the Loyalists. Although much research is needed to determine the extent of the slaves' impact in contrast to that caused by the influx of Liberated Africans who arrived between 1808 and 1860, from the evidence certain customs can be traced to the Loyalists' slaves. As demonstrated it is possible to trace Junkanoo back to the plantation. The slaves almost certainly practised bush medicine and identified with the black missionaries from their religion from America. Their story-telling, music and dance also have roots in the ante-bellum south.

An interesting study would be to determine which ideas and customs brought by the Liberated Africans reinforced those of the existing slave population and which were unique to themselves.

POLITICAL INFLUENCE[55]

The older white inhabitants disliked the newcomers. A feud developed between the Loyalists, the conchs and the established colonial administration. Gradually gaining prominence, the Loyalists caused the downfall of two successive governors, John Maxwell and John, Earl of Dunmore.

Becoming a party of opposition to the existing government in the islands, the American Loyalists criticised the administration. A Board of Loyalists headed by James Hepburn was formed in July 1784 wishing to 'preserve and maintain those Rights and

Liberties for which they left their homes and possessions'. It saw Governor Maxwell as incompetent and accused him of trying to withhold from them the right of trial by jury. Dubbing him a tyrant, the newcomers criticised Maxwell for surrendering the Bahamas to Spain and found fault with some of the local laws which they argued were unconstitutional.

Governor Maxwell dissolved the House in the face of scathing criticism and the outbreak of riots among Loyalists in Nassau. They resented seeing American ships in Nassau harbour flying the American flag. A new election was called in November 1784 and for the first time representatives were returned for Abaco, Exuma, Long Island, Cat Island and Andros. Previous to that date, only Nassau, Eleuthera and Harbour Island had returned representatives. In 1799 additional seats were created for Turks and Caicos, San Salvador, Rum Cay, Crooked Island, Acklins and Long Cay.[56]

The election of 1785 gave the Loyalists some members in the House of Assembly, but the old party was still in control. When several of the members who favoured the new party withdrew from the Assembly and persistently absented themselves because they considered elections unfairly conducted, they were expelled from that body. The Loyalists petitioned in May 1785 to complain that the House of Assembly was not constitutionally elected. Their petition however was not considered and is said to have been burned by the common hangman in front of the door of the House.

Although the House of Assembly was not dissolved between 1785 and 1794, the Loyalists gained ascendancy through by-elections. They owned more property than the older inhabitants and soon held the majority of the high positions in Government. The rowdy, troublesome newcomers, especially ringleaders James Hepburn, formerly Attorney-General of St Augustine and Robert Johnston, a Lawyer, successfully agitated against Governors Maxwell and Dunmore. Gradually the Americans became the stronger party in the Bahamas.

The American Loyalists greatly influenced political life. By their very numbers and their settlement in the Out Islands, they posed a challenge to the old order. The Government was almost forced to extend representation to the outlying islands. They no doubt had much to do with the purchase of the Bahama Islands from the Proprietors in 1787 and the purchase of a new mace for the House of Assembly in 1799.

Between 1784 and 1800, more laws which profoundly affected the social lives of the inhabitants of the Bahamas were passed. Included in the legislation were acts to reinforce the fledgling police force and a militia, to establish schools and to regulate fire protection and cemeteries. As discussed above, Acts were passed defining more stringently the colour bar. In the political sphere, the Loyalists passed legislation to limit the House to five years. Although this was amended from time to time, the Loyalist law was of some significance. The present day Parliament sits for five years.

Epilogue

Loyalist influence has been more far-reaching than was previously thought. The social, economic and political impact has been profound. Although the attempt to set up successful plantations failed, the social structure was changed by the newcomers and their slaves.

Quantitatively, there was a revolution in the Bahamas' population. The Loyalists set up many new settlements especially on the Out (Family) Islands and have left permanent imprints in the Bahamas on place names such as Glenton's Sound, and Buckley's Long Island, respectively named after Henry Glenton, Loyalist from New York and John Buckley, formerly a resident of East Florida. Moss Town, Great Exuma and Forbes Hill, Little Exuma were named after William Moss and Thomas Forbes respectively. Lyford Cay, western New Providence, was named after William Lyford, a Georgia Loyalist.

The enormous increase in the black population and the entry into the Bahamas of the energetic white merchants, planters and professionals, transformed the status quo. The new elements in the ruling class quickly consolidated their position and passed more stringent laws and regulations to safeguard it. They opposed amelioration of slave conditions and the ending of flogging of female slaves. The ruling class made sure that the black population, then in a majority, knew their place. The result was the hardening of racial barriers which was to affect Bahamian society for over a hundred and fifty years. Separated by colour and class, the division in the society was reflected in the cultural aspects of Bahamian life. While the powerful élite transformed the architecture of the town of Nassau where it lived and worked, it paid little attention to the over-the-hill or black section where the perceived social inferiors lived. The town of Nassau developed into a pretty and attractive city while over-the-hill, with little supervision, controls or planning, was left to its own devices, ultimately becoming a slum.

White Loyalists strove to improve the tone and literacy of Bahamian life by introducing a newspaper, a library and drama societies. At the same time the slaves perhaps imperceptibly passed on their customs such as Junkanoo and Obeah, with African origins but which were creolised.

In the economic sphere, the experiment in cotton-growing was largely a failure, although there is evidence that cotton production was revitalised in the 1860s on some Bahamian islands. Although the plantations failed, positive aspects emerged. The Loyalists, their slaves and their descendants learned to adapt to the lack of resources and the unyielding soil. They learned to survive as subsistence farmers and reinforced Bahamian industries which they had met, putting farming on a more stable basis. Shipbuilding, commerce, salt-production and to a minor extent, stock-raising also remained important to the Bahamas, especially in rural areas.

Politically, the Loyalists soon controlled Parliament. Their entry into the Bahamas brought wider representation with the increase of constituencies. Legislation was passed which reflected the hardening of racial lines, but which also made for social improvements, which mainly benefited the white population. Although much more research is needed, it is suggested that it was the Loyalist element which came to be the most influential in Bahamian politics, developing eventually into the Bay Street Boys who dominated Bahamian politics for generations. The Quiet Revolution in 1967 brought political and social change. The new politicians are mainly black and have roots in Africa and Europe. Interestingly, many can trace their roots back to the Loyalists and their slaves.

Notes

Chapter 1

1 Paul E. Albury, *The Story of The Bahamas*, London, 1975, p. 110.
2 Wallace Brown, *The Good Americans, The Loyalists in American Revolution*, New York, 1969, p. 2.
3 Ibid., p. 80.
4 Ibid., p. 81.
5 Ibid., p. 192.
6 William Wylly, *A Short Account of the Bahama Islands*, London, 1789, pp. 5-7.
7 J.D.Schoepf, *Travels in the Confederation 1783-1784*, Philadelphia, 1911, (reprint), p. 273.
8 William Wylly, op. cit., p. 3.
9 Ibid., p. 7.
10 Ibid., p. 4.
11 W. H. Siebert, *The Legacy of the American Revolution to the British West Indies and Bahamas*, Columbus, Ohio, 1913, p. 17. See also J. H. Stark, *History of and Guide to the Bahamas*, New York, 1891, pp. 172-173.
12 Maxwell to Sydney, 17 May 1784, C.O.23/25 pp. 104-105.
13 Maxwell to Sydney, 29 March 1784, C.O.23/25, pp. 76-77.
14 See Steve Dodge, *The First Loyalist Settlements in Abaco: Carleton and Marsh Harbour*, Occasional pamphlet by the Wyannie Malone Historical Museum, Hope Town, Bahamas, 1979.
15 Thelma P. Peters, The American Loyalists and the Plantation Period in The Bahama Islands, Ph.D. Thesis, University of Florida, 1960, pp. 62-63.
16 Ibid., p. 66.
17 Ibid., p. 22.

Chapter 2

18 Edward Brathwaite, *The Development of Creole Society in Jamaica 1770-1820*, Oxford, 1971.

19 See especially Michael Craton, *Searching for the Invisible Man. Slaves and Plantation Life in Jamaica*, Harvard University Press, 1978 and Barry Higman's 'Household structure and fertility on Jamaican Plantations: A Nineteenth Century Example', *Population Studies*, XXVII, 1973, pp. 527-550, 'The Slave Family in the British West Indies 1800-1834', *Journal of Interdisciplinary History* VI, 1973, pp. 261-287 and *Slave Population and Economy in Jamaica, 1807-1834*, Cambridge, 1976.

20 Thelma P. Peters, The American Loyalists and the Plantation Period in the Bahama Islands, Ph.D. Thesis, University of Florida, 1960, p. 122.

21 R.W.Fogel and S.L.Engerman, *Time on the Cross: The Economics of American Negro Slavery*, Boston, Toronto, 1974, p. 23.

22 See D. Gail Saunders, The Slave Population of the Bahamas 1783-1834, M.Phil. Thesis, University of the West Indies, 1978, pp. 459-461.

23 Michael Craton, 'Changing Patterns of Slave Families in the British West Indies', *Journal of Interdisciplinary History*, X:1, Summer, 1979, pp. 1-35.

24 Duncan C. Rice, *The Rise and Fall of Black Slavery*, London, 1975, p. 92.

25 The main secondary sources for this section are D. Gail Saunders, The Slave Population of the Bahamas 1783-1834, M.Phil. Thesis, University of the West Indies, 1978, pp. 62-63, 177-178, 307-311 and 426-437. See also Michael Craton's 'Hobbesian or Pangolossian'. The two extremes of Slave conditions in the British Caribbean, 1783-1834, *William and Mary Quarterly*, 3rd series, Vol. XXXV, April 1978, pp. 324-356 and his 'Changing Patterns of Slave Families in the British West Indies', *Journal of Interdisciplinary History*, X:1 (summer 1979), pp. 1-35. See also, Benson Mc.Dermott's, 'Lord Rolle', *Bahamas Handbook*, Nassau, 1981, pp. 14-32.

26 See D. Gail Saunders, The Slave Population of the Bahamas 1783-1834, op. cit., pp. 237-249, 311-314 and 433-434. See also Deans Peggs, *A Relic of Slavery. Farquharson's Journal for 1831-1832*, Nassau, 1957.

27 *Relic*, op. cit., p. 75.

28 Letter. Charles Farquharson to James Farquharson, 21 March 1832. O'Brien Collection, Public Records Office, Nassau.

29 Main sources used for this section were, D. Gail Saunders, The

Slave Population of the Bahamas, 1783-1834, op. cit., pp. 23-28, *Regulations for the Government of the Slaves at Clifton and Tusculum in New Providence*, printed at the office of the New Gazette, 1815, enclosed in Wylly to President Munnings, 31 August 1818, C.O.23/67 f.147, and *A Mission to the West India Islands Dowson's Journal for 1810-1817*, edited by A. Deans Peggs, Nassau, 1960, p. 61.

30 C.O.23/67/163a.

Chapter 3

31 Browne to Germain, 27 February 1779, C.O.23/24/61-62A.

32 Lord Germain to Maxwell, 9 November 1780. Enclosed in C.O.23/24/403-404. See also Michael Craton's *A History of the Bahamas*, London, 1969, pp. 157-158.

33 See Thelma Peters, The American Loyalists and the Plantation Period in the Bahama Islands, Ph.D. Thesis, University of Florida, pp. 148-149.

34 See *Bahama Gazette*, 14 January 1786 — 30 December 1789 and Craton, Ibid., p. 172.

35 *Votes of the House of Assembly*, 11 December 1787—18 December 1787, pp. 6, 19-21; 1 July 1791, p. 46, 10 September — 16 September 1793, pp. 5 and 12.

36 *Bahama Gazette*, 15-18 June, 1890, No. 332.

37 Ibid., 16-20 Dec., 1791, No. 488.

38 Ibid., 1 May, 1794.

39 D. McKinnen, *A Tour Through the British West Indies in the Years 1802-1803 giving particular account of the Bahama Islands*, London, 1804, pp. 170-171.

40 Ibid., p. 154.

41 Ibid., p. 160.

42 R. M. Martin, *Statistics of the Colonies of the British Empire*, London, 1839, p. 110.

43 *Bahama Gazette*, 12-16 February 1790, No. 297.

44 *Relic*, op.cit., p. 17.

Chapter 4

45 See Michael F. Doran and Renee A. Landis, 'Origins and Persistence of an Inner-City Slum in Nassau', *The Geographical Review*, Vol. 70, No. 2, April 1980, pp. 182-193.

46 Ibid., p. 189.

47 For more detailed information on this section see Gail Saunders and Donald Cartwright, *Historic Nassau*, London, 1979, pp. 11-24.

48 Ibid., p. 18.
49 Mrs Leslie Higgs, *Bush Medicine in the Bahamas*, Nassau, 1974, p. 1.
50 *Relic*, op. cit., p. 83.
51 A. D. Peggs, (ed.), *A Mission to the West India Islands. Dowson's Journal for 1810-1817*, Nassau, 1960, p. 36.
52 Information for what follows on the Methodists was obtained from an article 'The Spread of Methodism through the Bahamas' by Alan Betteridge in *Bicentenary Souvenir, Bahamas, Methodism in the West Indies 1760-1960*, pp. 10-20. The Baptist information was obtained from an unpublished paper 'Baptists in the Bahamas, Baptist Beginnings' by Antonia Canzoneri, soon to be published in the 1982 edition of the *Journal of the Bahamas Historical Society*.
53 See Clement Bethel's, Music in The Bahamas. Its Roots, Development and Personality, M.A.Thesis, University of California, Los Angeles, 1978, p. 87.
54 H. M. Bell, *Isles of June*, New York, 1934, pp. 161-162.
55 For more detailed information on this section see Wilbur H. Siebert, *The Legacy of the American Revolution to the West Indies and Bahamas*, Columbus, Ohio, 1913 and Thelma Peters, 'The American Loyalists in the Bahama Islands. Who they were.' *Florida Historical Quarterly*, Vol. 40, No. 3, January 1962, pp. 226-240.
56 40 Geo 111, C. 7.

Glossary

Ante-Bellum   before the American Civil War 1861-1865.

Cay   a low islet.

Cerasee (Momordica Charantia)   a quick-growing vine bearing bright yellow flowers and orange coloured seed pods. The plant is used extensively in the Bahamas as a tea for colds and fevers.

Commonage   the legal right of sharing land in common.

Conchs   a term meaning the old inhabitants of the Bahamas and their descendants, in contrast to the majority of the Loyalists on New Providence and the southern islands. Conch was the term also often used derisively towards the old inhabitants by the Loyalists. In modern usage it also means a white Bahamian.

Creole   slaves born in the West Indies or the Bahamas, as opposed to those born in Africa.

Driver   usually a slave who held the highest post of the field slaves. He was employed to oversee the slaves at work.

Droughing Vessels   boats which were used to carry produce between the islands.

Junkanoo   a festival brought to the Bahamas by African slaves and Liberated Africans. It is probably a corruption of John Canoe who was believed to be an African Chief in Axim Ghana, West Africa. Junkanoo is celebrated today on Boxing Day and New Year's Day.

Liberated Africans   African Slaves captured on ships after the abolition of the slave trade (1807), who were taken as prizes of war or seized as forfeitures and became the property of the Government. The Africans, on touching British soil, were freed but were boarded out as apprentices for periods of up to fourteen years. Many were

75

settled in villages or settlements such as Carmichael, Adelaide, and Grant's Town.

Lignum Vitae   hard wood.

Loyalists   Those who sided with the British in the American War of Independence. Also referred to as Tories.

Madeira   Bahamian mahogany.

Mulatto   the offspring of a Negro (African) and a person of European stock.

Osnaburg   a garment of coarse linen worn by the slaves. The word is a corruption of Osnabrück, a town in Germany renowned for its textiles, especially linen.

Out Islands   the term used until the late 1960s to describe the islands other than (or out of) New Providence.

Over-the-Hill   Those settlements or areas, which were predominantly black, south of Nassau and East and West Hill Streets. The areas include Grant's Town, Bain Town and Delancey Town.

Plaitters   Those persons (in this case slaves) involved in plaitting straw which could be made into baskets, mats and the like.

Quoins   Variegated stones used at the corners of stone buildings.

Rambling   wandering; in search of food and occupation which would include searching for wrecks.

Registration Period   In order to curtail smuggling the Imperial Government in 1816 requested West Indian Assemblies to pass registration bills. After a serious rift between the Executive and the Legislature, called the Wylly Affair, the Bahamian House of Assembly passed its Registration Act in 1821. Therefore between 1821-1834 the law required every slave owner to register his/her slaves.

Rushers   The people who take part in the Junkanoo festival rush, that is they do various steps to the music.

Salina   a natural salt pond.

Salt pans   in order to facilitate the natural formation of salt, salt pans, that is areas which were demarcated by stones, were made. As the salt was taken out, the pan was replenished with brine from the pond.

Salt-Raking   a process in which solid salt crystals are broken up and raked ashore in piles from natural salt pans.

Slash and burn   the method used to clear fields. The bush in chopped down and then burnt, and along with it a large part of the humus of the soil.

Triennial Return   The Registration Act passed in the Bahamas in 1821 established a Triennial Registration of Slaves in the Bahama Islands, that is slave owners were required to register their slaves every three years.

Watlings Island It is believed that Christopher Columbus landed at Watlings Island which is today known as San Salvador. Until 1926 Cat Island was referred to as San Salvador.

Wrecking an industry which was once legalised in the Bahamas. The salvage from wrecks was sold and wreckers received a proportion of the net proceeds.

Bibliography

Albury, Paul, *The Story of the Bahamas*, London, 1975

Bahama Gazette, 12-16 February 1790, 15-18 June 1790 and 16-20 December 1791

Bell, H. M., *Isles of June*, New York, 1934

Bethel, E. Clement, Music in the Bahamas. Its Roots, Development and Personality. M. A. Thesis, University of California, Los Angeles, 1978

Brathwaite, Edward, *The Development of Creole Society in Jamaica*, 1770-1820, Oxford 1971

Canzoneri, Antonia, The Baptists in the Bahamas. Baptists Beginnings. To be published in *Journal of the Bahamas Historical Society*, Vol. IV, No. 1, 1982

Craton, Michael, *A History of the Bahamas*, London, 1962

———, 'Hobbessian or Panglossian'. The Two Extremes of Slave Conditions in the British Caribbean, 1783-1834, *The William and Mary Quarterly*, 3rd Series, Vol. XXXV, April 1978, pp. 324-356

———, 'Changing Patterns of Slave Families in the British West Indies', *Journal of Interdisciplinary History*, X:1 (Summer 1979), pp. 1-35

Dodge, Steve, *The First Loyalist Settlements in Abaco: Carleton and Marsh Harbour*, Occasional Pamphlet by the Wyannie Malone Historical Museum, Hope Town, Bahamas, 1979

Doran, M. F. and Landis, Renee A., 'Origins and Persistence of an Inner-City Slum in Nassau', *The Geographical Review*, Vol. 70, No. 2, April 1980, pp. 182-193

Genovese, Eugene D., *Roll, Jordan Roll: The World The Slaves Made*, London, 1975

Governors' Despatches. C.O.23/25/folio. 76-77, 147, 163a

Higgs, Mrs Leslie, *Bush Medicine in the Bahamas*, Nassau, 1974

McCartney, Timothy, *Ten, Ten the Bible Ten: Obeah in The Bahamas*, Nassau, 1976

McKinnen, Daniel, *A Tour through the British West Indies in the Years 1802-1803 giving particular account of the Bahama Islands*, London, 1804

Martin, R. M., *Statistics of the Colonies of the British Empire*, London, 1837

Peggs, A. Deans, (ed.), *Farquharson's Journal or A Relic of Slavery*, Nassau, 1957

————, (ed.), *A Mission to the West India Islands. Dowson's Journal for 1810-1817*, Nassau, 1960

Peters, Thelma P., The American Loyalists and the Plantation Period in the Bahama Islands, Ph.D. Thesis, University of Florida

————, 'The American Loyalists in the Bahamas Islands: Who they were', *Florida Historical Quarterly*, Vol. 40, No. 3, January 1962, pp. 226-240

————, 'The Loyalist Migration from East Florida to the Bahama Islands', *Florida Historical Quarterly*, Vol. 40, No. 2, October 1961, pp. 123-141

Rice, Duncan C., *The Rise and Fall of Black Slavery*, London, 1975

Russell, C. Sieghbert, *Nassau's Historic Buildings*, Nassau, 1980

Saunders, D. Gail, 'The Slave Population of the Bahamas 1783-1834', M.Phil. Thesis, University of the West Indies, 1978

Saunders, Gail and Cartwright, Donald, *Historic Nassau*, London, 1979

Siebert, Wilbur, H., *The Legacy of the American Revolution to the British West Indies and Bahamas*, Columbus, Ohio, 1913

————, 'Loyalist Exodus to the West Indies: Legacy of Revolution, in *The American Revolution and the West Indies*, edited by C. W. Toth, New York and London, 1975, pp. 210-225

Schoepf, J.D., *Travels in the Confederation 1783-1784*, Philadelphia, 1911

Stark, J. H., *History of and Guide to the Bahamas*, New York, 1891

Wylly, William, *A Short Account of the Bahama Islands*, London, 1789